Welcome to
ST. AUGUSTINE

Dave Chatterton
General Manager

My HOMETOWN

WELCOME ABOARD! We are excited that you have chosen Old Town Trolley Tours to be your guide while you explore the Nation's Oldest City. Our expert tour conductors will entertain and inform as they navigate the trolley past the most significant points of interest, including historic homes, museums, grand hotels, beautiful churches, the Cathedral, and the oldest stone fort in the United States, the Castillo de San Marcos. Along the way the trolley will stop at 22 well-placed stops, which are located throughout the Historic District. This guidebook has been designed around these stops as a supplement to the trolley tour.

Throughout this guide book you will find arrows directing you to points of interest that can be found "off the beaten path," which you can explore by foot. While you are visiting you are welcome to step on and off the trolley at the designated stops. We encourage you to re-board the trolley at the same stop that you stepped off so as not to miss any of the tour.

The stop index and map at the back of the book allows you to quickly determine which stops are near which points of interest. While walking through our city, if you get disoriented, remember that the bay is at the eastern edge of the city and the Castillo de San Marcos (the fort) is to the north. You can use these landmarks to reorient yourself.

St. Augustine's History
A Brief Overview

▲ PONCE DE LEON

"In 1492 Columbus sailed the ocean blue." Everyone knows what happened next. He found a large landmass in the middle of the ocean, which would become America, and returned to Spain to report his discovery. On his second voyage across the ocean his first mate was Don Juan Ponce de Leon, who became the first Governor of Puerto Rico.

Tempted by legends of gold and a spring that brings eternal youth, eventually Ponce de Leon journeyed north from Puerto Rico. Very little documentation remains from this voyage, but one thing that has survived is a navigational fix taken by the world-renowned navigator, Anton de Alaminos, that puts them at 30 degrees 8 minutes north latitude, right in between present day Ponte Vedra and St. Augustine. The next day he stepped onto land and named it "La Florida" before continuing his exploration for treasures untold. While he never discovered the Fountain of Youth or gold, he discovered something that would become even more valuable — the Gulf Stream, a strong current that flows from the Gulf of Mexico up the east coast of the United States. This could shorten the voyage from the New World back to Spain by as much as three weeks.

Throughout the years there would be several attempts to settle Florida, but without success. The King of Spain had

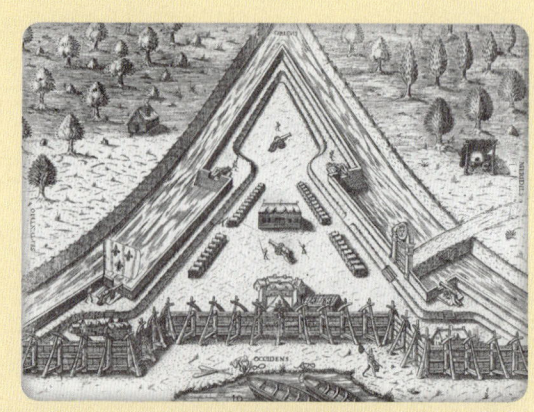

▲ FORT CAROLINE

decided that Florida was uninhabitable until a group of French Protestants, called Huguenots, succeeded in establishing Fort Caroline in present-day Jacksonville. This invasion of Spanish land infuriated the King, and he sent one of his best admirals, Don Pedro Menendez de Aviles, to rid his land of the Huguenots, establish a lasting settlement, and bring the Catholic faith to the natives.

Pedro Menendez landed with his army on September 8, 1565, and, after holding Mass, he began to accomplish his goals. He marched his men north toward Fort Caroline to attack

▲ **MATANZAS MASSACRE**

the French. Meanwhile, the French were sailing south to attack the Spanish. A terrible storm scattered the French army, leaving 250 shipwrecked survivors clinging to life south of the settlement where Fort Matanzas now stands. When Pedro Menendez and his men arrived at Fort Caroline they found it lightly guarded and easily taken. After extinguishing the French threat they returned to St. Augustine and went in search of the surviving French.

By the time the survivors were located they were hungry and exhausted. St. Augustine was a poor settlement without provisions to care for 250 prisoners. After determining that the survivors were Protestants and were unwilling to convert to Catholicism, Menendez had them put to the sword and their bodies dumped into the bay. The natives once called it the Bay of Dancing Dolphin, as dolphin can often be seen playing in the waters around St. Augustine. The massacre of the French gave the bay a new name: Matanzas, meaning slaughter or killing place.

The Gulf Stream made St. Augustine a valuable settlement that would become the last stop Spanish treasure ships would make before crossing the ocean. Because of this, St. Augustine came under attack many times. In 1586, the British privateer Sir Francis Drake attacked St. Augustine and burned it to the ground. In 1668, the city was attacked by pirate Robert Searles, who killed 60 settlers, prompting the Queen of Spain to order the construction of a stone fort to better defend the city. The Castillo de San Marcos was completed in 1695, and only seven years later St. Augustine would be attacked again, this time by Governor James Moore from Carolina. He burned the city to the ground during his 50-day siege, but was unable to take the Castillo. His attack led to St. Augustine becoming a presidio, or walled city. In 1740, General James Oglethorpe attacked the city, but he too was unable to take the Castillo and retreated after burning the south end of town.

▲ **1783 MAP OF ST. AUGUSTINE AS A PRESIDIO**

OGLETHORPE'S INVASION
(AS SEEN FROM THE CASTILLO DE SAN MARCOS)

GENERAL JAMES OGLETHORPE

In 1763, the British finally claimed St. Augustine, not by force but by pen. The 1763 Treaty of Paris gave Florida to the British in exchange for the return of Havana to the Spanish. During the Revolutionary War Florida remained loyal to the crown, but after the war ended a second Treaty of Paris returned Florida to the Spanish in 1784. In 1821, a peaceful transfer of power gave Florida to the United States. Florida became the 27th state in 1845.

St. Augustine changed forever in 1885 when Henry Flagler visited and attended Ponce de Leon Day, a yearly festival designed to draw visitors. Large Spanish ships would sail up to the town plaza and "Ponce de Leon" would step onto the seawall adorned with a uniform befitting the celebrated explorer. The entire town would flock to the plaza to be part of the event. There would be parades and costumed re-enactors bringing the event to life. Henry Flagler loved the experience and saw in St. Augustine the potential for a great resort town. That year he began construction on a hotel that he envisioned as the grandest in America. He purchased the small, worn railroads that led to St. Augustine and standardized the gauge. This allowed his guests to board the railroad in New York and ride it all the way to St. Augustine without having to change trains.

The Ponce de Leon Hotel opened in 1888 and made St. Augustine a tourist hot spot. While in St. Augustine, Flagler also built the Grace United Methodist Church in return for land so that he could build the Hotel Alcazar, which was home to spas, tennis courts, a bowling alley, and the world's largest indoor swimming pool of its time. He purchased the Casa Monica Hotel from Franklin Smith and renamed it the Hotel Cordova. He donated land to the Baptists so that they could build the Ancient City Baptist Church, and he donated money to the Catholics after the great fire of 1887 damaged their church. He also built the Memorial Presbyterian Church and today the mausoleum holds the tombs of Henry Flagler, his first wife, and his daughter, Jenny Louise, who is entombed with her day-old child in her arms.

Flagler continued his empire south, extending the railroad as he went. He eventually built the railroad all the way to Key West, a feat that no one thought was possible.

St. Augustine continues to be a popular tourist destination because of its dedication to the preservation and education of its past.

"The aspect of St. Augustine is quaint and strange, in harmony with its romantic history … It is as if some little old … Spanish town, with its fort and gateway and Moorish bell towers, had broken loose, floated over here, and got stranded on a sandbank."

-Harriet Beecher Stowe, 1873

HOTEL PONCE DE LEON
(NOW FLAGLER COLLEGE)

OLD TOWN

FREE PARKING | **TROLLEY STOP 1**

SAVE $$$ Buy your tickets from OLD TOWN TROLLEY

1a THE OLD JAIL - This served as the St. Johns County jail from 1891-1953. The building was financed by Henry Flagler so that he could control its look and location. He did not want it to be a blemish on what he considered to be his town. The Pauly Jail Company of St. Louis, Missouri, who also built Alcatraz, built this jail in 1891.

1b THE OLDEST STORE MUSEUM EXPERIENCE - The Oldest Store is arranged to look and feel like it did in the late 1800s when C. F. Hamblen first opened his popular business. Visitors are treated like customers, and museum guides act as storekeepers as they lead visitors around the store. On display are some of the most interesting products from that time period. The museum collection ranges from tonics and elixirs to a goat-powered washing machine.

1c ST. AUGUSTINE HISTORY MUSEUM - The museum is a combination of historical displays and private collections that bring over 400 years of Florida history to life. Guests can visit the Spanish sunken treasure room, a Timucuan Indian Village, and a Florida Cracker trading post.

1d GATOR BOB'S GIFT SHOP AND PENNY ARCADE - This is a place for visitors to purchase refreshments, souvenirs, and to play games.

 SHOPPING

VISITOR INFORMATION CENTER

TROLLEY STOP 2

The Works Progress Administration (WPA) built the Visitor Information Center in the Mediterranean Revival style in 1938. It's made of coquina, the same material that was used to build the Castillo de San Marcos. Here visitors can get an introduction to the city's history, buy attraction tickets, and obtain free information and brochures. The Visitor Information Center also offers special exhibits on the topics of history, art, and local interest. Check with the center for a schedule of upcoming events.

SAVE $$$ Buy your tickets from OLD TOWN TROLLEY

WELCOME CENTER U.S. 1 - This center is staffed with local professionals who assist visitors with everything from booking tours, making hotel reservations and getting discount tickets for local attractions, to providing you with area maps, brochures and more.
- 1305 N. Ponce de Leon Blvd / US1
- FREE PARKING and Complimentary Shuttle to Tour.

$AVE $$$ Buy your tickets from OLD TOWN TROLLEY

SAN MARCO HOTEL - On the property now occupied by the City Parking Facility once stood Florida's first grand hotel, the San Marco. The main structure was 260 feet long and five stories high. There were three towers along the front of the hotel. The tower in the center rose 131 feet. It is said that the tower could be seen 16 miles out to sea. It had its own theater, complete with stage, scenery loft and footlights. The San Marco was built three years before the Ponce de Leon hotel and featured electricity, steam heat, and Otis elevators. It was destroyed by a fire in 1897.

2a **PROJECT SWING -** Project SWING is the name of the playground behind the parking garage. SWING stands for St. Augustine's Wish for Its Next Generation. It was a community project in 1997, built by volunteers with volunteered supplies at no cost to the taxpayers.

FLORIDA CRACKERS - The term cracker came from the crack of the whip that was used by the Scots-Irish migrants who herded their cattle down to Florida as early as the 1700s. They would continuously travel the land, building Indian-style huts to shelter their families wherever they stopped. It was said you could hear the "crackin'" of their bullwhips a mile away.

WALK SOUTH

2b **SPANISH TRAIL MARKER -** Erected in 1928, this coquina ball is the Zero Milestone. It marks the eastern end of the Old Spanish Trail, the first transcontinental road from St. Augustine to San Diego, CA.

 **LOOK ONLY**

Potter's Wax Museum / Old Drugstore

TROLLEY STOP 3    **DISCOUNT PARKING**

George L. Potter's International Hall of Fame opened in 1949 as the first wax museum in the United States. The original figures were created by Gems, a popular wax studio in London, England and the costumes were certified for historical accuracy by the British Historical Society. Today, the museum displays over 160 wax figures of the people who created the history we study, the songs we sing, the books we read, and the paintings we cherish, the people who have contributed so much to what we are today. Potter's Wax Museum is located on the site that once housed the old Speissegger Drugstore.

3a **TOLOMATO CEMETERY -** The Tolomato Cemetery is the oldest planned cemetery in Florida. It has always been a Catholic cemetery, and is owned by Cathedral-Basilica Parish. Tolomato cemetery contains the oldest tombs with inscriptions in St. Augustine, with burials going back to the 1700s.

LOOK ONLY

3b **AUTHENTIC OLD DRUGSTORE -** Potter's Wax Museum is located on the site that once housed the old Speissegger Drugstore. The iconic building was constructed in cedar and cypress woods because of the material's resistance to humidity and rotting. In 1886, a doctor's prescription wasn't needed to purchase medicine. A druggist just mixed up something to make the patient feel better. Most medicine then was a mixture of grain alcohol, spring water and opium. It didn't cure anything, but the patient ended up not really caring.

3c **THE PRESIDIO -** Attacks on the city led to St. Augustine becoming a presidio, or walled city. A palm log structure running from the Castillo de San Marcos to the San Sebastian River was the northern wall of the city, called the Cubo Line of Defense. Reinforcing the walls were redoubts where soldiers could stand lookout and cannons would have been placed for defense against invaders. The Santo Domingo Redoubt stands at the intersection of Orange and Cordova Streets where the Cubo Line (northern wall) and the Rosario Line (eastern and southern wall) would have met.

CITY GATE

TROLLEY STOP 4

SAVE $$$ Buy your tickets from OLD TOWN TROLLEY

When the Spanish walled the city in the 1700s this gate was the only way in and out of the city to the north. The gate was locked every night at dusk and wasn't opened again until morning. Residents made it home on time or they slept with the snakes that night. The original gate was constructed out of palm logs. The current coquina pillars were built in 1808. One hundred years later in 1908, the city decided to tear the gate down, calling it an "eyesore." The Daughters of the American Revolution (DAR) protested, parking themselves in front of the gate in funeral clothes. They served tea and cakes to all passers-by, effectively saving the gate.

DISCOUNT PARKING

4a OLDEST WOODEN SCHOOL HOUSE - This attraction is located on St. George Street. It offers a look into how children were educated in the 18th and 19th century as it educated both girls and boys together beginning in 1788. The tiny building was built more than 200 years ago using red cedar and cypress, and put together using wooden pegs and handmade nails. The schoolmaster and his wife lived upstairs, above the small classroom. The building is encircled by a large chain, placed there in 1937, to help anchor it to the ground in case of a hurricane.

4b ST. GEORGE STREET PEDESTRIAN MALL -
St. George Street runs south from the city gate. There are over 25 buildings on this street that have been restored or reconstructed. It is comprised of retail stores, restaurants, and museums.

 SHOPPING

4c HUGUENOT CEMETERY - The Florida Territory was purchased from Spain in 1821, just in time for a virulent yellow fever epidemic to sweep through the city, depopulating it by one-third. The massive death rate from the yellow fever led to the establishment of the Huguenot Cemetery, a cemetery for non-Catholics. (Catholics were buried in the Tolomato Cemetery.) There are only a small number of headstones, but some of the graves contain as many as 25 bodies per grave.

 **LOOK ONLY**

Old Town Trolley Tours® of St. Augustine Presents...

GHOSTS & GRAVESTONES℠

Join us aboard the Trolley of the Doomed to visit two of St. Augustine's most haunted buildings. Reservations Required.

904-257-8211
GhostsandGravestones.com

COLONIAL QUARTER

TROLLEY STOP 5

St. Augustine's rich history is brought to life in this immersive journey through the centuries. Experience the Nation's Oldest City through interactive activities, living history demonstrations, and graphical stories. Visitors can take part in a musket drill, climb to the top of a replica of a 17th-century watchtower, dine on authentic 18th-century British and Spanish fare, and join the Colonial Crew Revue for an evening of lively historical information.

5a PIRATE AND TREASURE MUSEUM - This museum is stocked with over 600 real pirate artifacts and treasures on display. Visitors can learn about the pirates that plagued St. Augustine as well as other famous pirates from around the world. This is an immersive experience with the largest authentic collection of pirate artifacts in the world and more than 20 interactive exhibits through the Golden Age of Piracy. Experience the Disney-designed sound experience of Blackbeard's demise, fire a real cannon, and separate fact from fiction in the Hollywood Pirates exhibit.

PRIVATEER SIR FRANCIS DRAKE - Shortly after St. Augustine was settled, the city was attacked by the privateer Sir Francis Drake. He and 2000 of his men burned the city to the ground and chased everyone into the swamps.

PIRATE ROBERT SEARLES - The Castillo de San Marcos was built following a pirate raid carried out by Englishman Robert Searles in 1668. He burned down the ninth wooden fort along with half the city, and killed over 60 of the inhabitants. *(Image courtesy of the St. Augustine Pirate and Treasure Museum)*

5b CUNA STREET - Cuna Street is part of the area known as Colonial St. Augustine. There are shops, restaurants, and bed & breakfasts along the street.

 **SHOPPING**

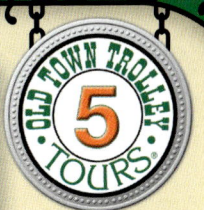

Matanzas Bayfront

TROLLEY STOP 6

The city is bordered on the east by Matanzas Bay. Before the Spanish began calling the bay the Matanzas, the Timucuan Indians called it The River of Dolphin because of the bottlenose dolphin that inhabit this estuary. The bay is also home to manatees, five different species of sea turtles, and more than 230 species of birds. The shallow salt-water marshes act as incubators and nurseries for fish, crabs, and oysters. This body of water is one of the most productive on earth. The inlet was originally farther south, near the lighthouse. In the 1940s the Army Corp of Engineers dredged a more accessible inlet during the expansion of the Intracoastal Waterway. *(Photo courtesy of Zach McKenna)*

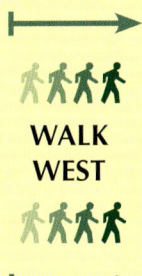

WALK WEST

6a CHARLOTTE STREET - Charlotte Street is also part of what is known as Colonial St. Augustine. It has always been an area that caters to shopping and eating because it was a straight trek for soldiers coming and going from the barracks to the fort. The street was named for King George III's wife, Charlotte. **SHOPPING**

For transportation to the **Alligator Farm** ZOOLOGICAL PARK and **St. Augustine Lighthouse & Museum**, and the Beach, as well as shuttle service from select hotels **Use the Old Town Trolley Beach Bus**

Complimentary with your tour. Beach Bus schedule located in the Sightseeing Map. Call 904-201-1277 for more information.

Hypolita and St. George Streets

TROLLEY STOP 7

The roads in the colonial sections of the city are very narrow and slightly curved. These design features were necessary for two reasons during the first Spanish period. One, the narrow roads funneled the sea breezes off the water and into the center of town, which even today provides natural air conditioning in this climate. Two, the narrow, crooked streets made an attack on the town much more difficult. Marching soldiers up these roads would be very hard to do.

$AVE $$$ *Buy your tickets from* **OLD TOWN TROLLEY**

ARCHITECTURE - The early Spanish colonists mostly built one-story houses with grass or palm thatch roofs and doors that opened onto a courtyard. After the city was destroyed by Gov. Moore of Carolina in 1702 the Spanish began using coquina to build their houses. When the British received all of Spanish Florida in 1763, they began to modify many of the houses. Doors that opened directly to the street were added as well as a second story made of wood, chimneys, fireplaces, and glass windows. In 1927, following the construction of a seven-story tall skyscraper, the city passed an ordinance that requires buildings to use Spanish Renaissance or British Colonial architecture that matches the historic look and feel of the city. There's even a height restriction limiting buildings to 35 feet. A beautiful result of this ordinance is the Hilton Hotel on the bayfront, which consists of 19 connected buildings made to look like homes.

 **WALK NORTH**

7a ST. PHOTIOS SHRINE - This site includes a shrine, a chapel, and the Avero house which was built in 1749 and restored in 1979. A tour of the museum features special exhibits that tell the story of the first Greek colony in the New World. This freestanding exhibit contains various artifacts, photographs, and historical documents. Inside the shrine are exhibits displaying the life of the early Greek settlers and the development of the Greek Orthodox Church in America. Nearby is the St. Photios Chapel, which is also open for visitors.

MINORCANS - Minorcans, Greeks, and Italians were brought from the island of Minorca by Andrew Turnbull in the 1760s to be indentured servants on an indigo plantation in New Smyrna. The plantation was a failure. In 1777, the starving survivors marched 60 miles north to St. Augustine. The Minorcans' continued residence here kept the city occupied after the British Period ended and the 2nd Spanish Period began. Had it not been for them, the city wouldn't be the nation's oldest continuously occupied European settlement.

7b PEÑA-PECK HOUSE -
The Peña house passed through several owners in its lifetime until Dr. Seth Peck purchased the former Peña residence and took over the practice of Dr. Andrew Anderson, a friend and associate of railroad magnate, Henry Flagler. For the next 94 years the Peck family continued to live in the house. Today, The Women's Exchange volunteers guide visitors throughout the house filled with Peck furnishings.

7c GRACE UNITED METHODIST CHURCH -
This beautiful church building is Spanish Renaissance Revival Style. It was built in one year (1886-1887). Initially, the congregation met on the site where the Hotel Alcazar (Lightner Museum) now stands. When Henry Flagler came to St. Augustine to build his resort, he sat down with the congregation of the church and offered them a deal: if they would sell their land, he would build them a brand new church. Architects John M. Carrere and Thomas Hastings designed the $84,000 church, whereas Flagler got property in return valued at $4,000.

7d ANCIENT CITY BAPTIST CHURCH -
Around the time the Grace United Methodist Church and the Flagler Memorial Presbyterian Church were being built, the Baptists were also in need of a church. They asked Henry Flagler for help and he offered to give them a piece of land if they would build a church on the site within two years. The congregation raised $10,000 and built the church within the specified time frame. Built in 1895 in the Romanesque Revival Style, the church is the first masonry Baptist Church in the state of Florida. **LOOK ONLY**

HENRY FLAGLER / STANDARD OIL - When Henry Flagler and partner John D. Rockefeller started the Standard Oil Company, Flagler walked the path from poverty to wealth. The death of his wife in 1881 and changes in big business practices influenced him to seek new challenges. A honeymoon stay at St. Augustine's San Marco Hotel with his second wife led to the formation of a friendship with resident Dr. Andrew Anderson. Anderson inspired Flagler's vision of transforming the old town into a winter playground for the rich. Flagler's hotels did more than change the city's skyline. He also developed a railroad, built churches, established a hospital, erected commodious homes for his business officers, and molded comfortable neighborhoods for his employees, thus leaving a permanent mark on the state of Florida. There is a statue of Henry Flagler at the entrance to Flagler College. It originally stood at the railroad station; it was later moved to the front of the Lightner Museum, then finally, in 1972, to its current location.

WALK WEST

7e SPANISH STREET - Spanish Street was known as the heart of the Minorcan Quarter during the second Spanish period. It's a great place to find a unique souvenir.

SHOPPING

Flagler Memorial Presbyterian Church

TROLLEY STOP 8

The Flagler Memorial Presbyterian Church was built in memory of Henry Flagler's daughter, Jennie Louise Flagler Benedict, who died after giving birth in 1889. Her infant daughter, Marjory, only lived a few hours. This is a Venetian Renaissance style building (designed by Ponce de Leon Hotel architects Thomas Hastings and John M. Carrere) modeled after St. Mark's Cathedral in Venice. The Venetian-style copper dome reaches 150 feet into the air. The Greek cross adds 20 more feet. The Church cost $200,000 to build, seats 600, and was completed in 1890. The construction only took 361 days. Inside the church is a specially-installed crypt containing the remains of Henry Flagler, his first wife, Mary Harkness Flagler (Jennie's mother), Jennie Louise, her infant child (in Jennie's arms), and one empty sarcophagus. The empty sarcophagus was for his third wife, Mary Lily Kenan. However, Mary Lily remarried after Flagler's death and was buried in her family lot in North Carolina. Henry had a son named Harry, who is buried in New York City.

TIFFANY GLASS - Prior to being contracted by Henry Flagler to install the windows of the hotel dining hall, Louis Comfort Tiffany had re-organized his company to specialize in glass for architects and builders. Installing the windows in the Ponce de Leon stimulated demand for his creations, making his name synonymous with excellence in glass. The 87 windows he installed in the Hotel Ponce de Leon are now valued at more than $100 million.

8a HOTEL PONCE DE LEON - This grand hotel had two firsts: running water and electricity, installed by Thomas Edison, in every room. A person had to be very wealthy to stay at the Ponce. All guests were expected to stay for the whole winter season with the exception of the following presidents: Grover Cleveland, William McKinley, Theodore Roosevelt, Warren G. Harding, and Lyndon Baines Johnson. The dining hall seats 600 people and is lined with Louis Comfort Tiffany stained glass windows. The ceiling inside the dining hall is painted with Spanish proverbs and pictures depicting the early history of St. Augustine. George W. Maynard, who painted the Library of Congress ceilings, was the artist. The Ponce de Leon Hotel was used as a Coast Guard barracks for trainees during WWII. The hotel closed in 1967 and the property was re-opened the following year as Flagler College. Initially, the school was a two-year, all-girl school, but by 1972 they were a co-ed, four-year, accredited institution. Today they have an enrollment of approximately 2,500 students. The building is open for tours daily.

8b MARKLAND, DR. ANDREW ANDERSON, AND THE ORANGE INDUSTRY - The Markland is one of the two remaining plantation houses in St. Augustine. Originally built in 1839 and continuously upgraded until 1900, it was the home of Dr. Anderson, who would become mayor and a generous benefactor of St. Augustine, commissioning works of art such as the two lion statues at the approach to the Bridge of Lions. The Greek revival mansion was designed by Thomas Crosby. Unlike other southern plantations, this property was not built on cotton. It was built on oranges, but oranges are not native to Florida. The Spanish introduced them to Florida, and they were so highly developed during the English occupation that St. Augustine was almost one continuous orange grove. While freezes were not uncommon, a bad freeze in 1835 ruined St. Augustine's groves. Another hard freeze in 1894 was the final blow.

LOOK ONLY

FLORIDA EAST COAST RAILROAD AND HOSPITAL - Henry Flagler had a problem when he began to build his hotels. How did people get to St. Augustine? Transportation was very poor with a choice of either horse-drawn carriage or steamboat. To remedy this he bought and rebuilt the railroad from Jacksonville to St. Augustine. In fact, as he expanded his hotel empire, he continued the line all the way to Key West, Florida. He was 82 years old when the railroad was completed on January 22, 1912. Henry Flagler provided health care for his employees at the Florida East Coast Hospital, where the St. Augustine Police Department is today. Health care was free for each employee, and cost 50 cents per month for an employee's family.

Villa Zorayda

TROLLEY STOP 9

The Villa Zorayda was built in 1883 in a Moorish Revival style, modeled after the Alhambra Castle in Spain. Franklin W. Smith was the architect and owner of the Villa Zorayda. The most important thing about the house was that it was the first building in St. Augustine constructed of poured concrete. At the time there were no cement mixers; these buildings were done by hand. Guided tours of the museum are available.

Lightner Museum

TROLLEY STOP 10

Now known as the Lightner Museum, the Alcazar Hotel was built by Henry Flagler shortly after he built the Ponce de Leon across the street. It opened on Christmas Day 1888. Henry Flagler built this hotel to provide informal entertainment to his guests. He built Turkish (dry heat) and Russian (steam) baths, a gymnasium, a bowling alley, billiard tables, and a movie theater where some of the earliest motion pictures were shown. The hotel also had the largest indoor swimming pool of its time. The pool and the Casino Ballroom both extended the width of the block. In the back, Flagler constructed four asphalt tennis courts, and that new-fangled sport of bicycling was introduced. *Hobbies* magazine publisher Otto Lightner bought the Alcazar in 1946. He used the building to store his massive collection of Victoriana and turned it into a museum two years later. Otto Lightner is buried in the courtyard of the museum. Today, relics of America's Gilded Age are elegantly exhibited on the museum's three floors. Costumes, furnishings, and other artifacts give you a glimpse into 19th-century daily life. Paintings from around the world are also on display. The museum features an extensive collection of music boxes, which are demonstrated twice daily.

10a CASA MONICA / HOTEL CORDOVA -
This hotel was named after the mother of Saint Augustine, Bishop of Hippo. Listed on the National Register of Historic Places, the Casa Monica Hotel is a majestically restored 1888 landmark. Franklin Smith built the Casa Monica using the poured concrete method that he brought to St. Augustine and a Moorish Revival style that gives the building the look of a castle. But with only three guests registered on its opening date, Jan. 1, 1888, Franklin Smith sold the building and all items to Henry Flagler for $325,000 only four months after it opened. Flagler renamed it the Cordova Hotel. It operated as the St. Johns County Courthouse from 1968 to 1997. The building was acquired by Richard Kessler in 1997 and completely renovated, reopening as a hotel on December 10, 1999. Today, after many changes, it has regained its original name, the Casa Monica. It remains a Kessler Collection hotel.

WALK SOUTH

10b LINCOLNVILLE -
Lincolnville is located in the southwest peninsula of the city. It used to be called "Little Africa." Emancipated slaves established the community in 1866 and it was renamed Lincolnville in 1878. It was a launching point for demonstrations that contributed to the passage of the landmark Civil Rights Act of 1964. A monument to these "Foot Soldiers" stands in the plaza today, and there are footsteps imbedded in the sidewalk to commemorate Dr. Andrew Young's perseverance and peaceful protest.

(left to right) Dr. Andrew Young, Dr. Martin Luther King Jr. and Dr. Robert Hayling in Lincolnville in 1964.
(Photo by Frank Murray.)

President Lyndon B. Johnson signing the Civil Rights Act of 1964

The Foot Soldiers Monument in the Plaza

10c DR. HAYLING'S DENTIST OFFICE -
Dr. Robert Hayling, a local dentist, was the local chapter president of the National Association for the Advancement of Colored People (NAACP) which organized meetings and peaceful marches. Their campaigns drew attention to activities in Saint Augustine and ultimately to the involvement of the Southern Christian Leadership Conference (SCLC) and Martin Luther King, Jr.

LOOK ONLY

10d CORA TYSON'S HOUSE - Mrs. Cora Tyson was a cafeteria worker in our local schools and a strong civil rights advocate. She opened her home to the visiting leaders of the Civil Rights movement, including Martin Luther King, Jr. Her family Bible contains a page where the signatures of her guests appear. An image of this page can be seen on a Freedom Trail marker in front of the house.

 LOOK ONLY

10e YALLAHA PLANTATION - There were many plantations in Lincolnville. The word "Yallaha" is the Seminole Indian word for "orange," and this was the orange plantation of P.B. Dumas, half brother to Alexandre Dumas, author of *The Count of Monte Cristo* and *The Three Musketeers*. With its layout and the wrap around porch, this home is one of the few remaining true British plantation houses in the nation.

 LOOK ONLY

ST. AUGUSTINE DISTILLERY

TROLLEY STOP 11

This building is the original home of the Saint Augustine Gas and Light Company, later to become Florida Power and Light. The Ice Plant was added to the northern end of the power plant and provided ice to Henry Flagler's enterprises and distilled water to his hotels and the Magnolia and Florida House hotels. In 2013 it became our first distillery in the city.

11a SOLLA CARCABA CIGAR FACTORY - The former Solla Carcaba Cigar factory is the oldest industrial building in Saint Augustine. Next to Henry Flagler, they were the second largest employer in the city; almost 90% were women. Although St. Augustine lost its tobacco industry to Tampa, at one time the combined production of the cigar factories here was five million hand-rolled cigars per year.

San Sebastian Winery

TROLLEY STOP 12

This building was initially offices for the Florida East Coast Railroad, but now houses the San Sebastian Winery. The San Sebastian Winery was opened in St. Augustine in December 1996 by Gary Cox and family. Given St. Augustine's vast and interesting history, it seemed appropriate to open the winery in a location near what history recalls as the birthplace of American wines. The winery offers a 45-minute free tour and wine tasting.

Whetstone Chocolate Factory

TROLLEY STOP 13

Henry and Esther Whetstone began their business in 1966 when they opened a homemade ice cream store on St. George Street. Today, Tedi's Olde Tyme Ice Cream remains a part of the Whetstone Chocolate experience. The Whetstones entered the chocolate market when they created a home-made fudge recipe. By 1967, they were selling 13 different flavors of fudge along with an increasing assortment of hand-dipped chocolates. In the early 1990s, the Whetstone Chocolate factory became a major attraction for tourists and local residents alike. Tours of the factory are offered daily and reservations are recommended.

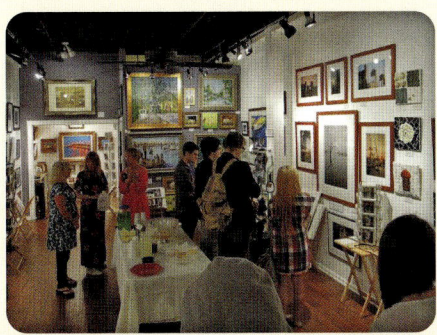

13a ART GALLERIES - St. Augustine has long been a Mecca for artists. Henry Flagler built artist studios at the Ponce de Leon Hotel to encourage artists to come here and create. There are numerous galleries throughout the city, many of which are on King Street. On the first Friday of every month St. Augustine hosts Art Walk. The art galleries are open later in the evening, and the community is invited to browse the latest exhibits. This is an opportunity to speak with artists and see what's new. Several of the galleries serve refreshments during this event.

SHOPPING

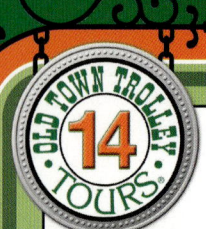

Cathedral Basilica

TROLLEY STOP 14

The Basilica de St. Augustine, the Catholic Cathedral, is the oldest congregation of any denomination in the United States. It dates from September 8, 1565. The St. Augustine Cathedral (now basilica) was dedicated on December 8, 1797, on the Feast of the Immaculate Conception. A fire gutted the cathedral in 1887. It was restored by the New York City architect James Renwick, who added the Spanish Renaissance-style bell tower. The church is 41 feet wide and 124 feet long with walls 24 feet high, to accommodate 500 people. In 1976, it was designated a basilica by papal proclamation due to its historical significance.

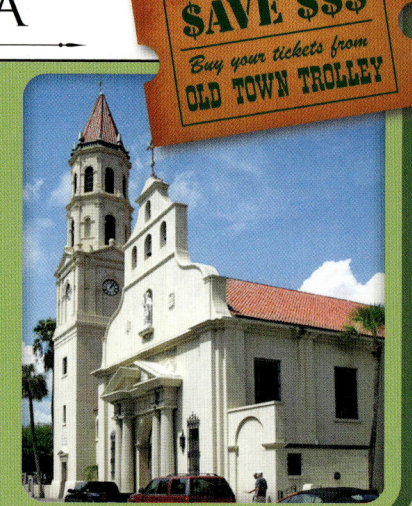

SAVE $$$ Buy your tickets from OLD TOWN TROLLEY

14a PLAZA DE LA CONSTITUCIÓN - In 1572, the Spanish king required that all Spanish colonial towns be built around a central plaza. They would have, at one end, a public market; at the other end, a government house; and a Catholic church that opened onto the plaza. St. Augustine followed this model.

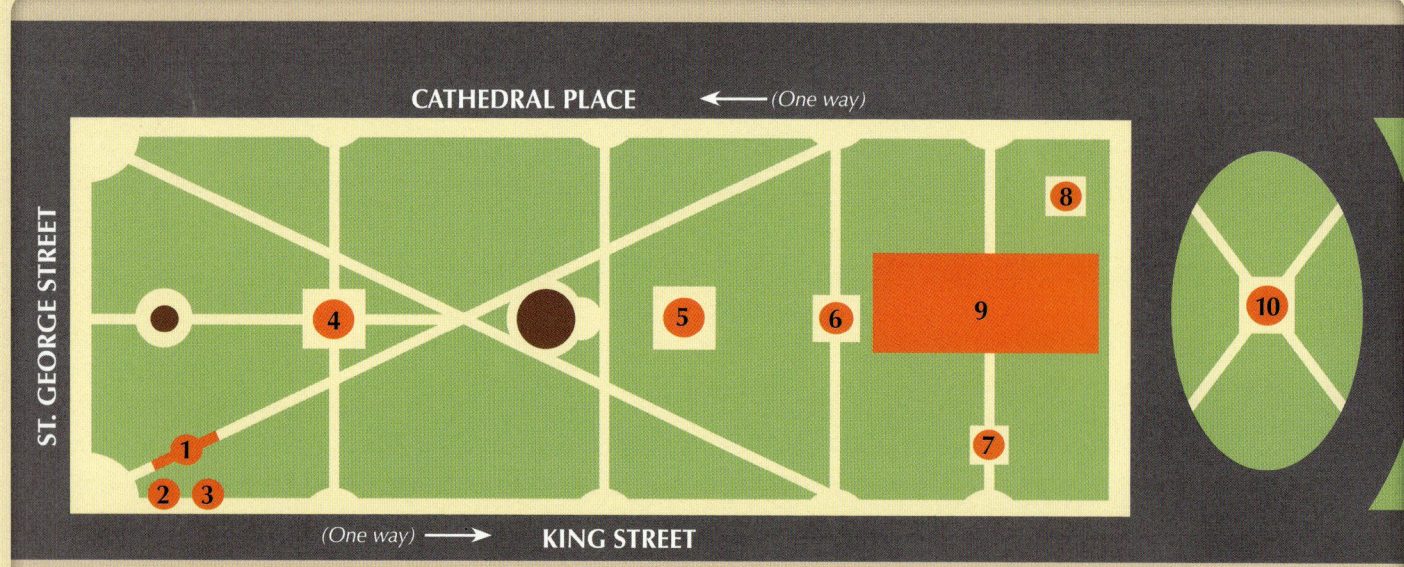

PLAZA DE LA CONSTITUCIÓN MEMORIALS AND MONUMENTS

1. The Andrew Young Walkway
2. Declaration of Independence Signers Plaque
3. Spanish Well
4. Spanish Constitution of 1812 Monument
5. Confederate Soldiers Monument
6. Public Well
7. St. Augustine Foot Soldiers Monument
8. Fallen Soldiers of WWII, Korea & Vietnam Monument
9. Public Market
10. Statue of Juan Ponce de Leon

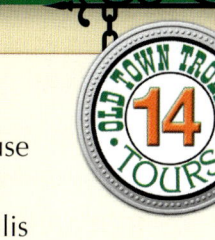

14b GOVERNMENT HOUSE - This building houses a city museum today. It was originally the government house of the Spanish, British, and American governments. St. Augustine acted as a port of entry to the US, similar to Ellis Island, during the 1870s.

WALK SOUTH

14c SOUTH ST. GEORGE STREET - A stroll down south St. George Street includes several structures worth noting. The coquina-constructed St. Joseph Convent is home of the Sisters of St. Joseph, who came here in 1866 to teach blacks freed during the Civil War. Other structures include the Villa Flora, a Moorish and Romanesque Revival residence, and the Stansbury Cottage, or Gingerbread House.

14d TRINITY EPISCOPAL CHURCH - The cornerstone for the Trinity Episcopal Church was laid on June 23, 1825. The church is an example of a Gothic Revival building and is decorated with beautiful Tiffany-style stained glass. This is the oldest Episcopal congregation in the state of Florida. Visitors are welcome to walk through the church if the door is open.

Aviles Street / Beach Bus Stop

TROLLEY STOP 15

The Beach Bus runs every hour on the half hour. It takes guests to beachside hotels, as well as the Alligator Farm and the St. Augustine Lighthouse & Museum. Access to the Beach Bus is included in your trolley ticket. To purchase your trolley ticket or for more information about the tour, call 904-201-1277.

→ 🚶🚶🚶 **WALK SOUTH** 🚶🚶🚶 →

15a AVILES STREET - Aviles Street was one of nine original streets in the town plan, which was mapped out in the 1500s according to Spanish requirements for colonial towns. It is often referred to as the oldest street in the nation. Today, the street is active with shops, restaurants, and museums.

SHOPPING

15b THE ST. AUGUSTINE HISTORICAL SOCIETY RESEARCH LIBRARY - Built in the late 1700s, the first known resident of this house was Bernardo Segui, a baker from Minorca who supplied baked goods to the soldiers at the fort. This Spanish colonial building was later the birthplace of famous Civil War General, Edmund Kirby-Smith, the last Confederate general to surrender, and his slave Alexander Darnes. Darnes later became the first black physician in Florida. The building was used as the public library from 1896 to 1987. It is presently the research library of the St. Augustine Historical Society. The library is free for those wanting to do research.

15c XIMENEZ-FATIO HOUSE - This house is a museum focusing on the property's role as a boarding house run by Miss Louisa Fatio starting in 1850. This was one of the few socially acceptable business ventures for a woman living then. The colonial house is open for tours and is impeccably restored to give guests an authentic look at colonial living in a boarding house at the time. Miss Fatio continued the inn until her death in 1875. The property was owned by Miss Fatio's heirs until 1939, when it was purchased by the National Society of The Colonial Dames of America. It stands as one of the best-preserved of the three dozen colonial buildings remaining in St. Augustine. The historic grounds of the museum date to St. Augustine's original town plan of 1572.

SURPRISE STORE - St. Augustine had its own version of Walmart way back in 1887 in the form of the Surprise Store. It was located at 1 King Street, where A1A Aleworks is today. It was called a "dry goods and clothing outlet" and was owned and operated by J.W. Estes. In the late 19th Century it was the largest department store on the east coast of Florida. According to the *Tattler* (the early version of the *St. Augustine Record*), no stranger visited the store without expressing surprise.

15d SPANISH MILITARY HOSPITAL MUSEUM - This reconstructed building is a one-story Spanish-style structure with rooms arranged in a ward atmosphere depicting a hospital. This museum is situated atop the coquina footprint of the original hospital. The museum shows how the hospital would have been in 1791, complete with furnishings, herbal remedies, tools of the trade, and a look at the daily life of a wounded or sick soldier and his caregivers.

OLDEST HOUSE

TROLLEY STOP 16

This is the oldest house in St. Augustine, not the United States. Because of a devastating attack by Governor Moore of Carolina, there are no houses in St. Augustine that predate 1702, and the Oldest House was built sometime after that date. This Spanish Colonial house is known as the Gonzalez-Alvarez house. The five flags hanging outside the Oldest House represent the five periods of St. Augustine. The St. Augustine Historical Society maintains this complex, which is open to the public.

16a ST. FRANCIS BARRACKS - The barracks are the headquarters of the Florida National Guard. This building was used originally in the First Spanish period as the headquarters of the Franciscan mission. The British converted the mission to military use and it has served as a military base ever since, with 2015 marking its 100th anniversary.

 **LOOK ONLY**

WALK SOUTH

16b NATIONAL CEMETERY & SEMINOLE WARS MEMORIAL -
Just south of the St. Francis Barracks is the National Cemetery, which is open to the public and has a memorial to the soldiers who fell during the 2nd Seminole Indian War. This was a very difficult war for St. Augustine. The Indians eventually surrendered, nearly starved, and were transported to Oklahoma, except for those that escaped into the Everglades swamp. The Indians that never surrendered to the federal government can still be found in the Miami area today.

TAKE THE BEACH BUS TO ANASTASIA ISLAND

16c ST. AUGUSTINE LIGHTHOUSE & MUSEUM -
A Spanish watch tower was built in the late 1500s. It was converted to our first lighthouse in Florida in 1824. However, by 1870, the tower was threatened by shoreline erosion, so construction began on the current lighthouse. In 1876, a brick light keeper's house was added to the site. The old tower succumbed to the sea during a storm in 1880. The current tower was built in 1874. It is 162 feet high with a beam visible 19 miles over the water's surface. There are 219 steps up to the top. Constructed of Alabama brick and Philadelphia iron, the lighthouse is St. Augustine's oldest surviving brick structure. At the top, a first order Fresnel lens serves as the beacon. This tower was automated in 1955. In 1980, the Junior Service League of St. Augustine, Inc. began a 15 year campaign to restore the tower and keeper's house, which were destroyed by fire in 1970. The house was opened to the public as a museum in 1988. In 1993, the tower was also opened to visitors on a daily basis.

RETURN ON THE BEACH BUS

16d BRIDGE OF LIONS -
Constructed in 1927 to reach Anastasia Island, the bridge was completely re-done between 2005 and 2010. Originally, it was simply referred to as the "Matanzas River Bridge." The city issued a $1 million dollar bond to pay for the bridge, which spans 1,545 feet from shore to shore. Today, the name "Bridge of Lions" comes from the two lions that are on display at the approach to the bridge from the west side. These lions were a gift to the city from Dr. Andrew Anderson. They were sculpted from Carrara marble (the same quarry that Michelangelo used), and anchor this historic Mediterranean Revival-styled bridge that spans the Matanzas River between St. Augustine and Anastasia Island. The lions were made to resemble the Roman lions at the Loggia de Lanzi in Florence, Italy. This very scenic bridge was not called the Bridge of Lions until 1928.

16e **TREASURY STREET -** This thoroughfare is the narrowest street in the city. In the earliest plan of St. Augustine all the streets running east to west were this size. The streets were designed this way as a defensive measure in case the city was attacked from the water. This method also assisted in cooling the buildings by accelerating the sea breezes, in accordance with Bernouli's Principle.

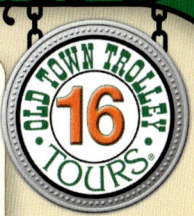

Castillo de San Marcos

TROLLEY STOP 17

Prior to the construction of the Castillo, St. Augustine was guarded by a series of nine wooden forts that proved inadequate for the task. The Spanish queen authorized the building of a stone fort, and construction began in 1672. It was completed in 1695. The cost of building the fort by today's standards would be between $30- $35 million. It was built to protect treasures carried by the Spanish ships from pirate attacks. The fort has never been taken by force. It is the oldest masonry fort in the United States.

COQUINA - The fort and quite a few other structures throughout town are made from coquina, a rock that is naturally formed in the ocean from limestone and fossilized shells. Coquina is very soft when first quarried, and so is left to dry for one to three years before use in building. Coquina was handy to build forts with because the heavy cannon balls would sink into the coquina instead of fracturing or breaking the structure. The native Americans in the St. Augustine area as well as the Spanish settlers would make a material very similar to coquina, called tabby. Tabby has the same elements that coquina does: water, sand, lime, and oyster shells, but it is made by hand, not by nature. Though not as strong as coquina, tabby could be used to build houses and even defensive walls. The Spanish learned that they could use it to make a formidable wall by leaving the sharpest edges of the oyster shells sticking out toward the enemy. A good example of tabby can be seen surrounding the Fountain of Youth.

→ 🚶🚶🚶 **TRAVEL NORTH** 🚶🚶🚶 →

17a FORT MOSE - In an effort to attack the British wallet, the king of Spain allowed safe haven for any slaves that escaped to St. Augustine. All they had to do upon arrival was become Catholic, and the men had to join the militia. By 1738, there was a large enough population of freed slaves to support the establishment of Fort Mose. It became the first line of defense from the north. The fort was located about two miles north of what is now the Old Jail.

→ 🚶🚶🚶 **TRAVEL SOUTH** 🚶🚶🚶 →

17b FORT MATANZAS - Fort Matanzas National Monument was built in 1742 to defend the city of St. Augustine from British attack and to guard the southern approaches to the city. Five cannons were placed at the fort - four six-pounders and one 18-pounder. All guns could reach the inlet, which at the time was less than a half mile away. The fort is accessible only by guided boat tours, so visitors must take a short ride on a passenger ferry. All tours and events are dependent on the weather.

RIPLEY'S BELIEVE IT OR NOT! MUSEUM

TROLLEY STOP 18

Robert Ripley traveled all over the world and collected many different weird and bizarre objects that are on display here. After he died his heirs purchased the Warden Castle Hotel and, in 1950, opened the first Ripley's Believe It or Not! Museum in the world. The museum is noted for its collections of unusual artifacts.

18a WARDEN CASTLE - Built in 1887 as the winter home of William Warden, a business partner of Henry Flagler and John D. Rockefeller, this Moorish Revival style mansion was known as the Warden Castle. It was one of the most striking private residences in the city. In 1941, the castle changed hands and was remodeled as a hotel by Pulitzer Prize-winning novelist Marjorie Kinnan Rawlings and her husband, Norton Baskin. Rawlings was the noted author of *The Yearling* and *Cross Creek*.

WELCOME CENTER

SAVE $$$ Buy your tickets from OLD TOWN TROLLEY

DISCOUNT PARKING — **TROLLEY STOP 19**

The Welcome Center is a great place to get information about the city, buy attraction tickets, and plan your stay. This is also the starting point for Ghosts & Gravestones®, voted best ghost tour in St. Augustine 2010, 2011, 2012, 2014, 2015, 2016, 2017, 2018 and 2019.

19a UPTOWN SAN MARCO - The various shops in this area carry everything from clothing and antiques to beads and stamps. On the last Saturday of each month, the San Marco Merchants Association runs the Uptown Saturday Night event. The stores stay open late to showcase their merchandise. Refreshments are usually served, and some places have live music.

🛍️ **SHOPPING**

19b ABBOTT TRACT HISTORIC DISTRICT - This area features 124 historic buildings within 17 blocks. The district has the highest percentage of pre-1930 buildings in the city. It was the site of the first real estate development outside the colonial city. The area was developed by Lucy Abbott of Charleston. She began development in the 1860s and is credited with 129 homes in the area. All but five still stand today.

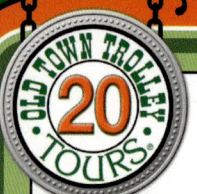

Mission Nombre de Dios

TROLLEY STOP 20

These grounds are the home to Mission of Nombre de Dios. There is a free museum on the property, as well as a bronze plaque that memorializes 45 of the 200 missions established in St. Augustine's First Spanish Period. Bishop John J. Snyder, Bishop of St. Augustine, dedicated the plaque in May 1996. Back in the woods is an old Catholic Cemetery. Some of the headstones have "USCT" on them, which stands for United States Colored Troops, referring to the black soldiers who fought in the Civil War.

20a THE GREAT CROSS (BEACON OF FAITH) -
The cross was erected by the Diocese of St. Augustine in honor of the 400th anniversary of the city. It is 208 feet tall and weighs 70 tons. It marks the landing site of Pedro Menendez de Aviles and commemorates the first Catholic mass.

20b FATHER LOPEZ STATUE -
A statue of the priest who accompanied Menendez when he landed in St. Augustine is located on the bayfront as you approach the Great Cross. Father Lopez can be seen with outstretched arms, recreating the pose he would have used when he celebrated the first mass.

20c THE SHRINE TO OUR LADY OF LA LECHE -
The shrine is located towards the back of the mission property in a wooded area across the water. Our Lady of La Leche is the first Marian shrine in the United States. Translated, the name means "Our Lady of the Milk." Marian shrines are sites that are centered on a historically strong devotion to the Virgin Mary.

OLD SENATOR

TROLLEY STOP 21

In the center of the Villa 1565 Hotel (formerly Howard Johnson) parking lot is the Old Senator, St. Augustine's oldest living "citizen." He was here for the Timucuan Indians, Juan Ponce de Leon, Pedro Menendez de Aviles, Henry Flagler, Dr. Martin Luther King Jr., and now you. This large live oak tree is 13 feet around and more than 600 years old. It is called a live oak because its leaves are always green.

21a MAGNOLIA AVENUE - This street is lined with Florida live oak trees. *National Geographic* magazine called it one of the ten most beautiful streets in the country. The canopy of branches has formed over the street in response to constant sea breezes blowing from the east. Enhancing the canopy is the Spanish moss that hangs from the branches.

SPANISH MOSS - The gray, stringy plant hanging from the oak branches is called Spanish moss. It is neither Spanish nor a moss but an air plant. Although it is attractive to look at, it's usually loaded with bugs (red bugs or chiggers). Henry Ford used it in some of his first Model T's to stuff the seats, causing the first automotive recall in US history.

WALK NORTH

21b FLORIDA SCHOOL FOR THE DEAF AND BLIND - In 1883, Florida's legislature established an institution for the blind and deaf at a cost of $20,000. They requested bids from various towns in the state for the location to build the School. The city of St. Augustine offered the best bid with $1,000 cash and five acres of land. The first three wooden buildings were originally built at a cost of $12,749 and were completed in December, 1884. By 1892, there were 62 students enrolled. Ray Charles attended the FSDB between the ages of 8 and 15 years old. **LOOK ONLY**

Fountain of Youth

TROLLEY STOP 22

The Fountain of Youth Park is the site of many archaeological discoveries of national historic importance, with new excavations intermittently under way. The property was once home to the ancient Timucuan Indians, and evidence of several early Spanish forts has also been found on the property. A planetarium on the grounds illustrates how the Spanish used the stars to navigate the seas. Visitors can taste water from a re-creation of what Ponce de Leon believed to be the Fountain of Youth and can walk out on the 600-ft.-long observation platform over the marsh. Re-enactors roam the property, and cannon firings and demonstrations are ongoing throughout the day.

PONCE DE LEON - Fifty-two years before St. Augustine was settled, Spanish Explorer Don Juan Ponce de Leon was arriving in Florida. Natives had told him of a fountain to the north that had the ability to grant eternal youth. He went in search of this fountain, said to be located on the island of Bimini, and instead arrived in what is now Florida.

TIMUCUAN INDIANS - Archaeological digs have determined that the Timucuan Indian village of Seloy was probably located on the Fountain of Youth site. Wars with the Europeans and other native tribes, as well as a smallpox epidemic decimated the tribe. It is believed that those who survived the smallpox may have joined the Seminole tribe; however, the Timucuans were not the ancestors of the Seminoles.

For transportation to the **Alligator Farm Zoological Park** and **St. Augustine Lighthouse & Museum** and the Beach, as well as shuttle service from select hotels Use the Old Town Trolley *Beach Bus*

Complimentary with your tour. Beach Bus schedule located in the Sightseeing Map. Call 904-201-1277 for more information.

HISTORIC TOURS OF AMERICA
The Nation's Storyteller invites you to

VISIT US IN THESE FINE CITIES:

KEY WEST
Old Town Trolley Tours®
Conch Tour Train
Key West Aquarium
Key West Shipwreck Treasure Museum
Harry S. Truman Little White House
Cayo Hueso y Habana HISTOREUM®
Sails to Rails at Flagler Station
Mallory Square℠ Festival Marketplace
Dry Tortugas National Park Ferry
Yankee Freedom III
Ghosts & Gravestones℠ Tours
Key West Walking Tour
Shops at Mallory Square

SAN DIEGO
Old Town Trolley Tours®
San Diego SEAL Tours
Old Town San Diego Market
Ghosts & Gravestones℠ Tours
La Jolla & Mission Beach Tours
San Diego City Lights Tour

BOSTON
Old Town Trolley Tours®
Boston Tea Party Ships & Museum®
Ghosts & Gravestones℠ Tours

SAVANNAH
Old Town Trolley Tours®
Ghosts & Gravestones℠ Tours
Ghost Town Trolley
American Prohibition Museum

WASHINGTON DC
Old Town Trolley Tours®
DC Ducks
Monuments by Moonlight
Arlington National Cemetery Tours
Washington Welcome Center

ST. AUGUSTINE
Old Town Trolley Tours®
Old Jail
St. Augustine History Museum
Ghosts & Gravestones℠ Tours
Oldest Store Museum Experience
Potter's Wax Museum
Gator Bobs

NASHVILLE
Old Town Trolley Tours®
Soul of Music City Night Tour

1 (800) - TOUR-HTA
1 (800) 868-7482
HISTORICTOURS.COM

100% SATISFACTION GUARANTEE

EXPLORE AMERICA

TRUSTED TOURS & ATTRACTIONS

Trust us, we've been there! We visit and review our members for quality, content and value. And best of all eTickets purchased with TrustedTours.com are backed by our 100% Satisfaction Guarantee.

Planning your next vacation? Visit TrustedTours.com today.

TrustedTours.com

100% MONEY BACK GUARANTEE

CLICK. PRINT. PLAY!

Old Town Trolley Tours® of St. Augustine Presents...

GHOSTS & GRAVESTONES℠

Join us aboard the Trolley of the Doomed to visit two of St. Augustine's most haunted buildings. Reservations Required.

904-257-8211   GhostsandGravestones.com

Old Town Trolley Tours, Transportainment® is a registered trademark of Historic Tours of America®. **Ghosts & Gravestones®** and **Frightseeing®** are registered service marks of Historic Tours of America®.

© 2021 Historic Tours of America®
ISBN - 978-0-9729463-9-1

Designed and Compiled by Historic Print & Map Company 1/21 10M
85 Riberia Street • St. Augustine, FL • 904-824-5908 • www.historicprint.com